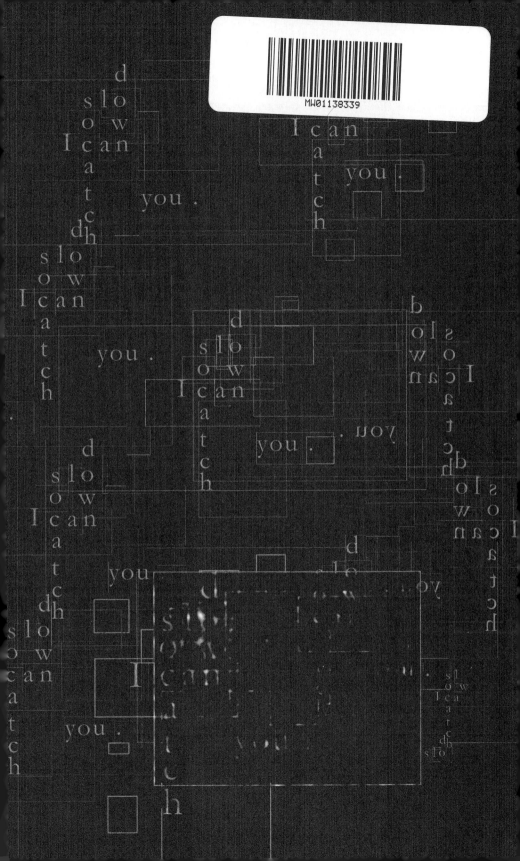

Traces of a Fifth Column
Copyright 2017 by Marco Maisto
ISBN: 978-0-9970932-5-4
All rights reserved

Book design and layout by Lawrence Eby
Cover art by Paul K Tunis
http://paulktunis.com/

Printed and bound in the United States
Distributed by Ingram

Published by Inlandia Institute
Riverside, California
www.inlandiainstitute.org
First Edition

Traces of a Fifth Column

Marco Maisto

To the girl at the zine shop

Contents

Tape

But we always make love with worlds.

-Deleuze & Guattari

[This work is] subject to weathering,
which should be considered part of the piece.

-Robert Smithson,
from a note accompanying *Partially Buried Woodshed*, 1970

[movie-theater firstbase hula-hoop throwing star

[annotated field guide]

for more information

                                        please scream

      they'd rather curse
      the dark

                                          the ones that tilt at
                                        spirals

                than replay
                the tape

     I say the day is more sonorous

                      when

                                          it is
                                        relived
                                        in real
                                        time   .

The Octavo of Human Landscapes

(ante di

luv

ian

alia——)

[*Picture of a crowd*
that looks like a snake
made of a crowd, goes here.]

When we were young, wasn't this the only way to get around that felt right? When we swam across that flickering cyanotype campus like ghosts looking for the edge of autumn; when we were palimpsests incredulous of grasses and solid obstacles. When we learned how to live two lives at once. Back then, when we respected each other's right to become scenery. Back then, when we respected each other's right to become scenery.

I found the notebook in the guestroom of the guesthouse.

Urgent cursive on the cover reads, *The Octavo of Human Landscapes & Homecoming Emergency Tones.*

Scratched into the front matter, a double-epigraph, half in a handwriting I recognize, half in one I've never seen.

I see where he'd cut out the most of the pages with an X-Acto knife, shuffled them out of order, then bound and joined them to the spine with glue. *People say he would fold intimate messages into technical writing that only she would know how to decipher.*

In all blank books, the amount of leftover pages is a kind of message. His, sprinkled throughout, tell the story of a summer that had sprouted its own heartbeat, and was now interrupting his final conversation with the person he knew he would soon cease to be.

I read your notebook out loud. I see your descenders become heat lightning. I hear his voice coming to life in mine. *I feel your words throwing fists in my mouth:*

The Octavo of Human Landscapes

&
Homecoming
Emergency
Tones

"How your name remains tattooed below the faded tan line on my hipbone. Z. No longer part of the Icelandic alphabet, and hasn't always been the final letter of the English. Once, it was second to last, followed by an ampersand: like this chiasmic attempt to return to where we started—&, &, &, &."

"I can hear you howling far off. Spines
grow from my spines. We are hordes.
Let's descend on a village."

—*Toward a Theory of Ampersand as Gyroscope*

&

&

&

&

(Day 72)

I step into the grain elevator half expecting my name to fall off. These are the plaids of my countryscape: easy blues and buckwheat blurs. This is my skeleton. Whale ivory mixed with landlocks, hay, soy. My name falls off.

"How many horses can you fit in a thumbprint?"

I know her the way I know the contents of a rattle. *Green confetti filling my head and ghosting out thoughts.*

(Day 1)

sneakers bubblegum lightbox bandana earthquake .

(Day 105, Instant Island)

Dear Yellow-Green Cambridge Cotton Fruit, Dear Card Trick, Dear Delicious Record Climate, Dear Story-About-a-Boy-That-is-a-Story-About-Two-Boys, Dear Ampersand as Drilled Thing, Dear 13th-Floor-Floating-Plastic-Bag, Dear Warning, Dear Disclaimer, Proclaimer, Dear Geodesic Honeycomb, Dear Table, Dear Table of Contents,

This is how I am. I'm a lot a lot a lot of unnamed layers shuffled by an oversexed regional holiday ghost whose glands have evolved to serve up safe, sane visuals that you can infest in one bite.

Today was aftermaths; I saw what the flood left behind. Or more like what it *didn't*. My letter beginning, "you will never have to drive here," should be amended to say, *"you will never be able to drive here, no one will."*

Writing in italics by hand. Becoming-invisible girl. Calling a bluff.

"Feminine, marvelous and tough."

When you are a part of every most important thing that happens in a place, gets to be you understand that place from a sort of cosmic perspective—but no other. I *am* as a map *feels*.

Dear Mirage, let's face it, we're a universal establishing shot. Natch, for this bifurcated black & white movie laced with instructions for how to walk through walls. Opening sequence: eyes that eat jump cuts, mouths around a flame in front of a backyard tent set. Dear Pixel, dear damp, broken Calendar Pulp.

(Day 1,500,000)

fair skin zine shop galaga-green wheat field

see-thru girls driver's license anti-paper fringe science
midtown rain delay laboratory understory
land mind tank girl oh I see eye ball
tennis court tennis court tennis court tennis court
dry heat low branch soda-hurts honey cream
cliffnotes love ya art directrix driveway wolf
cleavage-sand white flag sand bar blood oaths
Math Park expo long drink psychic death
pixie cut lemon juice electric tape anarchist
whale skirt memory plant stage magician mushroom cloud
horror books Manic Panic Tascam 4-track

iced tea zine shop long legs ragnarok

(Day 33)

Dear Crazy Avenue, Dear Informatrix, Dear Crusader's Chocolate, Steam Engine, Dear Sex on Easter, Dear Corner of My Event Horizon, Dear Cinnabar, *Dear Entire Alphabet—*

I built heavy triangular meditation modules in the megabrambles to remind me that the people I meet (that I meet without you to ground me) are more than just my inner experience of this place given form.

I read your journals: *every color matches every color.* I hammered you into my own work:

Sculpture Composed of Time Machine, Various Reds Things,
& Women in the Periphery Who Turn Out, Yes, to Be You

Two figures sit on an embankment overlooking a petrified week. One points at the steepest slope and whispers into the other's ear. *Time is in fact a spectral band,* where greys contend with golds and blues, where residual hums force your name into my mouth, the way nervous girls treats a pocket designed to hold all things secret. See reverse.

(Day 45)

She patented his handwriting, deciduous neon on red grass.
She registered it as an aqueous solution.
She registered it as a technique.
She registered it as a multiplex.
She registered it as a ghost town.
She registered it as the heartland.
She registered it as a breed.

I collected grass stains today for you. I know the tricks that all boys do.

(Day 118)

hot homemade movie
cassette-tape grey orchid
horizonless footnote
torch party orchid
heart-attack leafpile
so I can catch you
irrepressible measure
so I can catch you
who are you not
navy blue halfday
torch-party driveway

lean closet blindfold
telepathic yours truly
virtual taupe
improvised ochre
virtual taupe
who are you not
irrepressible measure
nervous thirdperson turnpike
who you've illusioned
stunning blue hammock
rope-burn romantic
last-chance grey dress
telepathic and wasted

starter home rain spout
who are you not

cassette-tape grey lips
color-drunk codeboy
virtual taupe
erasure-grey landscape
is it all that bizarre
it's really bizarre
throat-closing square knot
an overlooked thing
Jurassic-green raincoat
so I can catch you
starter home rain day
perfect host body
yours truly host body

(Days 50-51)

Instant   island   .

(Day 700)

Dear Japan, Dear Ambient Author, Dear Oh, Dear Transfiguration Boy, Dear Chemical Girl, Dear Fiber of my Fire, Dear Big Red Scarf, Dear Halloween Buoy,

Desire & lists.

The idea of me—the hash-marked outline that universally precedes my body by mere moments—writes this to you. It will say everything I need it to, but usually not in the order I want it to.

Today I am contumbled lists: immobile butterfly building, hand town, hand-to-hand town, butterfly more building than. *I am recursion*, it says.

I am captions: Afterimage shortcutting through a sunsetting wind farm. Shadow planting deciduous neon messages in hungry white grass. An earth's first words. Semi-organic things we've used for shelter. *I am a still life with red gems, supermoon, and blood-fiction.*

I am modes of transport. *I am a stamped envelope with a black mirror inside.*

I want elegant longhand, like yours. I want to list all the things I plan to steal from your future self—*the one I picture sitting beside me, on a train hurtling toward the first time we are to meet.*

(Day 11)

She drank a whole tank of diesel and the leaves returned to their trees. I belong in this country about as much as any far-afield ginkgo does. I was the parachute-bud grace note stuffed where golden hues dangled down.

Look: my whitest eyes.

These are the bulbs of your origin story: a raptor-staring-at-the-wall kind of story, a substitution-by-coronation story. A park-skirt story. A tsunami tent story. A memory bunker story. A you and you and you and me and it story.

(Day 25)

Your everyday fires want you back.

(Day 111)

Dear Exorbital Fangirl, Dear Double-Blind Bind, Dear Open-Label Test of Faith, Dear Birdsmouth, Dear Similar Notch in Other Components, Dear Boy in the Back Room, Dear Halogen Swimming Pool, Dear Constant, Dear Constant, Dear Painless Aura, Dear Metallurgist, Dear Ampersand-Monologue,

> *Paint me where the tan on your hips used to be.*
> *Attach me to the motion-lines in the last panel. I*
> *want the last trace of your disappearance to be the*
> *thing that puts me in quotation marks.*

Instead of you, I'm left with miniature plasma reactor hums coming from the bedroom. Do I remember the moment I forgot who I was? Do you? Miniature quantum tectonic events pass between us like sharpened butterfly murmurations.

There's an ultraviolet crease in the cassette tape spewing from my mouth. The longer I remain in this place, the more my story becomes yours.

Like us or soap or a boat or a season, these notebooks have minds of their own. The one you're holding now came with someone's handwriting carved into the first page. It reads: *The people you love become trade routes tattooed across your body, and tearing yourself apart is how you keep them alive.*

[(   )]

dear book, dear armada of your chest, dear finch-colored echo, dear other book.

(Day 2)

Dear Ochre Oleander, Dear Heartbeat, Dear Blonde Avalanche, Dear Drunken Summer Gravel, Dear Hide-&-Soft, Dear Raft, Dear Crystalline Z, Dear Teary Peninsula, Dear Fractal-Silo, Dear Secret Voice, Dear Bluest Bird, Dear Barometer, Dear Poisoner's Explanandum, Dear Unfixed Depth-of- Field, Dear Field-Within-A-Field,

Let's say *never*, but mean *later*.

(Day 365)

Words that bludgeon. Lions that collapse. Dust that settles.
Plush, plural, feral & with you in the tub.

The only way to forget his letters is to write over them. Let me show you how.

(Day 5)

[great plains states, icy elbows, [   ], flagless pole.
autumn-thunk thoughts grow winter spines,
    in this sketch of your
        flickering anti-neighborhood:

burnt leaves, [   ] water, [   ], liquid blackbirds,
obstruction only tongues can remove—.

crises on infinite earths, [   ], chances,
[ ] chants, flatbed-shout, & vermillion small-town fear,

          my halves
        of our things,

              go   here.]

Stunned into the fractal optics of the night, I nearly forget
what I came here for. The drawing above reminds me.
Supine strokes weigh on one another like palms. Both
kinds of.

*He's standing between the darkened zendo and her three-story
apartment house. She tears through the foliage and onto the
street. Their names fall off.*

I came here for more.

(Day 701)

Gasoline harbor   trampoline   aplomb   a-bomb.

Fog so thick
you live in
the moment.

(Day 49)

I tell you about foreign places that I don't really believe exist:

Auckland
Oshkosh
Tibet
Truth or Consequences
Brixton
Brighton
Kerry
Odessa
Santa Fe
Kiev
Brittany
Osaka
K'un-lun
Tyrol
Trieste
Zanzibar
Big Sur

My impression of each place is the sum of my feelings about its name, that bundle of fleeting associations and dissolving pictures that falls to the ground when I shake the word by its trunk. Kent: mint sprigs over the back of a horse cutting through fog toward the grave of her one true rider. Dover: when the air tasted the way blue paint does, licked off a bleached seashell.

(Day &—)

Dear Heresy-Star, Dear Other Side of the City, Dear Alternate Ending, Dear Your-Hair's-Other-Color, Dear Bicycle, Dear Missing String, Dear Soda-Fountain Suicide, Dear Annihilation Wave, Dear Anamorphic Ampersand, Dear Toy Boat Hollyfuck Anarchist Stapled Book Black Hole & Other Ways Around History,

The movie opens with you standing in chaff. Black/tan post-harvest light leaks. Plastic Halloween-pumpkin, quantum earthquake, heroin. Polaroid. Orange balloon, teal sky, antimatter-bomb. Smile. Ok. Click. Invasion.

As evr, Click.

(Day—)

cassette-tape grey hips
cassette-tape grey hips
cassette-tape grey hips
cassette-tape grey hips
cassette-tape grey hips
cassette-tape grey hips
cassette-tape grey hips
cassette-tape grey hips
cassette-tape grey hips
cassette-tape grey hips
cassette-tape grey hips
cassette-tape grey lips

nervous thirdperson turnpike
nervous thirdperson turnpike
nervous thirdperson turnpike
nervous thirdperson turnpike
nervous thirdperson turnpike
nervous thirdperson turnpike
nervous thirdperson turnpike

an overlooked thing
an overlooked thing
an overlooked thing
lean closet blindfold
an overlooked thing
an overlooked thing
an overlooked thing
an overlooked thing
an overlooked thing
an overlooked thing
an overlooked thing
an overlooked thing

(Day 13)

Reverse-process dynamite in the rose vase.

(Day 90)

I have pushed
　　　　solid staccatos
　　from my mouth
out the window
　　　　down onto
　　pixelated Midwestern sidewalks
dressed up in birds
　　　　　　challenged by arcade chemicals
　　that demanded
　　　　more self-possession
　　　　　　　　than I came here
　　grafted-to.

　　　　Look really close

he's holding a postcard,
　　reads: *Towel warmed on oven door to not-freeze.*
　　　　I homecome more complicated.
　　　　　　　　This will take time.

(Day 0)

Math, math, math, math, math, maths. We're now past the vanishing point and into an aftermath. At first, there's a fold in the sky. Next, a ghost in the leaves. Finally, a letter. Irradiated wrapping-paper dressing up an S.O.S. My letters fasten lightning rods to our new syntax.

Flat induction antennae. Flat interception umbrellas. Hand-to-hand town. Butterfly more building than. Bottle-at-sea-with-a-handgun-inside.

Communication has become the echo of dissolving planets. *Skirt-plummet green.* Endgame-white tonguekiss. I design colors for things that don't have any. Navy blue halfdays, salty red heat-spikes, Jurassic-pink rain delays. I distill younger, northeastern summers into lists. Pinecone, Sno-cone, skateboard, comic books, handjob. Gluesticks, warm-buzz, laser-light, tunnel-fort. Heliotrope extremophile, ocean-trench hand gesture. *Dear brand new mainline, dear sentient style,* I miss you in the tendons and find you in the absence thereof.

(--———--)

[hello   foxdogs   this is
       esteemed   coneyislandbunny   hello
              magnet   this is   estimable
   seafoam   black   rainjacket
              hidon'twait   OK   wait
      hi   magenta   hand   hot glowseas
   mindsharing-hot   foam
         mountianfoam   hi foam left by
   soft machinic   drawings   of   34
      hand-recognizable   hand   gestures
                     [   ]
      signaling   thinking   auburn   grasses   OK?
              OK   holdme   losslike,
   goes to her   there glass & mirror   comes to me
                                                 here.]

"All evening and stunned into the hem of the night, I forgot what I looked like."

The last line of the notebook reads like it ought to be the first. It promises a story about daydreams mapped onto waking life, dream-language onto actual talk.

The sketch on the book's endpaper, reproduced above, seems out of place: fat rendered from images and left bubbling and viscous at our feet. Spattered with impurities, it seems to diagram the differences between the deep-sea creatures of drunken summers we'd somehow survived, and the specters of ourselves that swim still, in the underground aquariums of summers rapidly to come.

Tape

Tape

[picture goes here.]
[fractured shadows in the day go here.]
[statue goes here.]
[photograph goes here.] [parachute goes here.]
[picture goes here.]

[*monolith-halos and
their terrible shadow*

go here.]

but we believe in a cure for thought.

in ossifying,
telepathic syntax.

you want newer old things.

TVs that cycle through gradations
of fissured sky, dissolving genius tree canopies on

every channel.

I want a tiny device that lets me walk through walls
at the cost of one randomly-selected memory.

desire will be the beginning of us.

It frees us from one another's arms and
pulls sun into the bedroom. I and
I & I will muffle longitudes in exchange for a graceful machine.

car money snacks mixtape gun

front porch opium thigh-freckles carpet bomb

[Human island underwater green-
gray grooming green to grass now
back to gray now back to green
escape-hatch green I'm back to grass
and   back to grey—I'm
                    I   am   alone.
I'm midnight gray—a grocery store
green grocery store oh now I'm yes
oh back to yes—I'm back to red yes
backup red—yes black to red and
yes back to grey—I'm back to—.]

I found the tape. The smudged date
had been written in his hand, the
tightly-kerned label in hers:

Fall-time & the Seduction of Dusks

"The first things we lose are the
wispy, zero-dimensional things:
memories of glances, plumes of
freezing breath—dissolvable things
we take for granted, even though
they're more precious than anything
on earth. Unholdable things, like
the tiny parts of speech we can't
picture—things behind things."

Her free hand had opened the stereo
door. Burnt ochre hair tumbling
across her face, she pushed the

tape inside and pressed PLAY. It was her own voice, talking about Christmas trees on the deck of a whaler. Sea winds, followed by the sound of a hand, firmer than her own, stopping the recorder.

sleeper hit   sleeper holds   out-of-state rules

coffee sugar succulent sunrise handgrenade .

[breadcrumbs leading
back to a story
not yet told
start here.]

The pixilated fabric fragment explains all of this. Its unfixed edges
say something about at the last hands that held it.

Same as the directional symbols stamped along its warp—blooming,
still-damp electrical storms that they are. *Flag-within-a-flag.*

Snow that won't stick. Traces of a fifth column.
Hay-bale red diagrams that show us how we must configure our fingers

if we're going to filter driveway torches from the new salvos. The cloth's
only word doubles as an action-word. Our word

nails messages to ghost buildings in the rain.

• • •

Look: semiprecious stories become raspberry thigh-stroke stories.
Histories of sunflushed, autonomic weekends

in whole months without espionage—days that'll chase you.
The choices before us have outlines

and moor well in color clusters:
vocations that can revise gravity,

tradecraft that can blow up a sun.
Gazing up: interzonal fricatives, like helicopter buds,

swan-dive into your open, unsure hands.

• • •

Now we've got to weave ourselves into this thing's weave.
Add stories to its story: *The Night We Coded Dusk Into The Street.*

Who We Are to Each Other. Our word collects dissolving footprints, it
traces trick doors in chalk along blind alleys when the city floods.

Our word is a texture-word.
I could decipher the swatch with it, but you do—

I am the gunmetal coating her dress, the assassin's hem.
I am the line that sinks in. I am so much raveling sloeberry dew

turned bitter ink.

rock paper scissor fist time bomb

reading list absinthe tan lines tripwire

[a futurist goes here.]

I know this window:
traced-city window
last window on earth

   archipelago window ::

you

tattoo it

on my line of sight

        (:: you paint radio broadcasts

behind an electric blue Japanese dressing screen)

and even though a discussion
with the wall

is now possible

we   hold   out
for the end   of the spiral   .

I am becoming the impurity in your mission

the color that makes your color incomplete without another.

you listen

to perendinating,
alarmist radio, you sell me on

        snowdays   of the mind

      & tricked-out   almost-narrative,

   play-by-play surveillance— .

the kitchen windows are cold, starting to buckle.

and in the whiteout 6 stories down,

we watch

motel-red streetlamplight and rooftumbling metonyms

fill up our eyes and our mouths.

[.]

kirby krackle from the window plants   ::   sleep, and terse/laconic overkill.

I want an ultimate nullifier.
and spoken, dog-eared stories—.

I want

to wear the heart's face
between this blizzard   and that blizzard.

        and even supine,

you want omissions we can feel and
watch on the news—you want to be
the very first impurity
to climb between
        a woman and a man and a woman and a man

        pantomiming winter mercies

in a glowing window
pages away

from this one.

red house watertower paperback birthday fuck

electric fan doctor strange sour cherry avalanche

[Humming photograph of a geodesic butterfly house goes here.]

I can't remember who shot the footage, but I know it could have been me. Perhaps especially because no good can come of it, I play the tape again:

1.   *Prehistoric habitat inside a glass room.*
2.   *Arrested waterfall, light that scatters funny.*
3.   *Giant red Paleozoic moth explodes from megaflora.*
4.   *My name falls off.*
5.   *Moth dives toward camera.*

I hit PAUSE before the creature can burst through the TV screen. I rewind the tape. I rewind the tape more.

This story is an event horizon that only days ago engulfed another version of myself whole and entire. I am bait for worlds. I am mercy. I am joy. I am honey in the maw of an unhinged reality throbbing at the edges of this viewfinder you've bolted to my eyes.

[one has the urge or an inclination or feels the necessity to or a compulsion] calla lily sundown short-shorts hair-needle nootropics

[a missing piece goes here.]

dear werewolf-zazen inducer, dear heart-attack leafpile,

I want   more   bands   of slow motion between us   .

dear grass-stained-kneetops-
where-mouths-should-be, dear

overactive mirror, bursting
        with licks of condensed breath,

dear countryside
made of empty windows, dear

electrode-flowers and April-at-night: I want

bright blue polygraph shavings, and
cassette-tape grey lips;

radiation you can hold like a baton—
        anything that can   rain   through you   .

I want, or I want to be,
the device-part of your mind—

the part oscillating between emergency tones,
the one sending out rogue signals that bounce

against the sporadic partition between
you and you and you.

last call zen center strange bed short hair neutron bomb

skin tint thindex waterflower bombpop

[*slaws of plosives*
and *kissing mechanism* go here .]

[This is the spot where we draw the outline of a conversation

    about spontaneous drowning.

Starlings
    beyond the bluest starlings,

        aeroplanes
        in the ocean,

    and thoughts
    within thoughts,

        all show up.   ]

    your lines converge here. at me.
    arrows take me from behind.
        the soft morse-code machine come to life:

the fringe

of this co-located-and-dissolved-space

between alternate titles,

is the sweetest space.

you look up at me

"the divine countenance,"
you say,

the divine countenance

is clever
at maddening

and driving
all souls out of their senses

in longing for it   .

[after-image of two figures
proudly presenting—
  like a prized mackerel—a 3D print of
their esteem
        for each other

        (its radial symmetry

in the first weeks
        of its joyful gushing-up)

                dwindles here.]

rooftop pickup truck museum-nymphomaniac

hopscotch pitfall jeopardy risk—kinesic day pass like little lifetimes we believe in the deep efficacy of crushing waves

that we've learned
to kick back and forth
just before

      the frame freezes.

also in waves
beneath waves

and erotic vivisections—

we talk dirty along
the railing.

it mumbles

wet electric stones
back:

knit aquamarinelife.
seawater tapestry.
telekinetic light. dusk.

I murmur blood magic into your ear:

you don't exist
the proof of you doesn't exist.

liberated particles. salt air. sodium light. dusk.

you don't just get to just desire me
you get to have to tear apart the
landscape that enfolds me.

string-theory. paraffin. new straw. old broom. strings.

we blur at the shore.

desire   it's

        a honeycomb

made   of
gazes

seducing the spiral.

        glances.

                something that finally

        passes between us   .

smoke that stands for fire
and is a fire.

waves.   and more than.

listen.

their perfect parasol diction.
loud in the bluster

[./]

hear it and know

    that they are building you.

a better you—

    fevertrees
    sprouting

from
your mind.

[   ]

film stock
    and grain blow through my face,

turn hair
into math.

it might as well be dusk you say it stands for
dusk all this stands for fire for fire
at dusk.

"the tides aren't where they should be."

[   ]

I start to say something
about how salt air + you—

                                        but you've already
                                        tasted me.

            "the blue light
            sounds greener here."

            I watch your back for
            dangerous byzantine sealife.

new wave light. solid sea.
psychic nets. psychic death.

we play a zero-sum game
at the edge

of an echoless beach.

young man, shave-ice, psychic death: the Midwest

trampoline gasoline seaside-plummet VCR

bedroom tape:

      they forget
            their desires—

        the ones who trace at sundogs—
           and are left with the desire to desire—

        my entrance confuses
        the plummet.

    all hiding places

   reveal a God   whose omissions

       [   ]

     they've
          yet to realize, even
       as She runs

into their lap,

          sun-vexed
       by the erasure.

we all
look

  for the smoke-tail

    of something sharp

      with living edges

        leaving the sky

        for some

          new and dark

          gathering storm

            amid opalescent abutments   .

a fission-haired wild flower surfaces here.

dear book, dear armada of your chest, dear finch-colored echo, dear other book

[a notebook bound with cassette tape closes here.]

I was the dark form

tied off

by the colored strings
of someone else's

strange garland.

I was the difference
between the echolocated thing

and the mold of it

you hold close.

I was a room where questions
became sculptures.

you were the passive voice,
expressed
as

tactile enhancements,
homesick, haptic feedback:

consolation

for the shell
that used to make sense here,

brackets that we once fit inside.

I was the table

where our words would be scattered
until forgotten

and—in one version—
stumbled-upon.

data recovery comes to an
end that way—

you talk in your sleep.
images slip off of things.   future summers

swim

toward the shutter.

an empty city
has grown between our words,

and running through it
on all fours

is an unholdable girl.

[The loneliness of *a middle distance
transmissions aggregator* is pinned here.]

This all begins
with a massive scribble over our unraveling self-portrait

you've got a black hole in your hands

you bow
to the last of the blue TV-screen light
at the end of our bedroom video

it starts late in the apartment

you blush

with asterisks
at the edges

of your mouths

every year is contained
every   year   is contained
in this nighttime.

all the time we're cold

told the leaves turned—
all at once—
weeks ago

we are   constantly   rewound

and passed along   .

I keep all of your thumbs
between us—

the triptych you sleep in—
blue lights on blue lights on blue lights—
your smooth handmade ellipses

the ceramic guest check—

metempsychotic half-lifer,
I blur the room

make noises with my mind.

how can we protect our friends
from their exploding bookshelves?

from outthinking their reflexes?

if all nocturnal gardens are ours,
and the bluest bird is ours,

and the escape hatch in the Buddha's head,
and the Catskills and internal Christmas lights are ours—

if the seasons are contumbled
if ropes have fallen from the atmosphere—
then we are now

on another earth.

incense Converse
frenchkiss EMP   .   ]

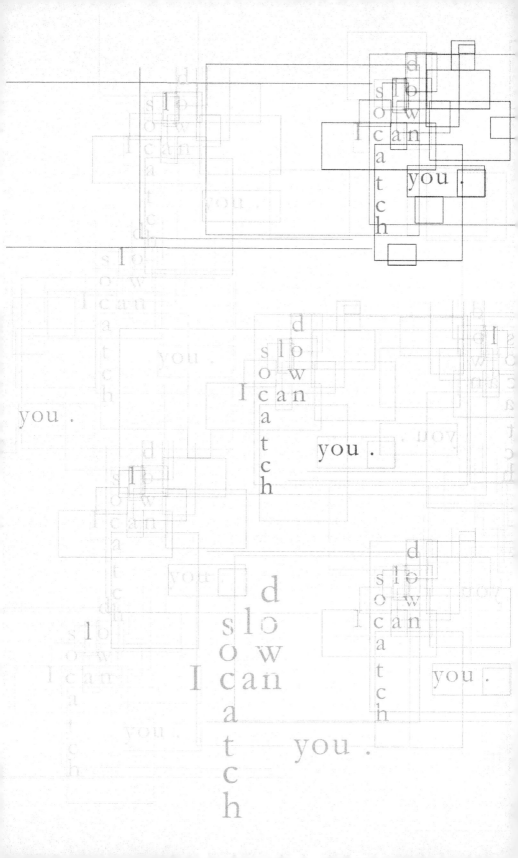

Acknowledgements

This book would still be several milk crates full of murmurs and trouble if not for the kindness and brilliance of more people than I can name in this space. By a longshot.

Still, I want to offer my deepest gratitude to Greta Byrum, Claudia Rankine, Mary Margaret Sloan, Sal Randolph, Richard Kostelanetz, John Goslee, Andrew Sulllivan, Morgan Vo, Michael Chaney, Ravi Shankar, Erica Mena, Adam Clay, Ed Skoog, Travis Sharp, Aimee Harrison, Rob MacDonald, Dara Cerv, Ali Power, Ralph Hamilton, Kirsten Miles, Adam DeGraff and Tyler Burba—all friends, teachers, or persons responsible for bringing the finest poetry to the public.

And to Carrie Bennett, Broc Russel, Dina Hardy, Laura Sims, Cole Swenson and Anselm Berrigan, for their feedback and massively inspirational style.

And to Matt Kindt and Jonathan Hickman for their work and worlds.

And to my whole family.

I also owe special thanks to Caroline DeVane, Jame Slotta, Alissa Larson, and Don Brunjes, who were essential writing and art partners during the time *Traces* was taking shape.

And to the people who have literally made this book possible: Cati Porter, an extraordinary publisher full of kindness; Lawrence Eby, the immensely talented designer of this book and a true creative partner; rob mclennan who gave the collection a chance; and to Paul K Tunis, about the best comics poetry creator on the planet: I gave Paul a rough manuscript and he gave me back insanely evocative, arresting, and tender cover art.

Finally, my irreducible gratitude and affection go to Leah Margaret Galey, who is inextricably bound up in this book.

Notes

The line, "Feminine, marvelous and tough," on pg 14 belongs to Ted Berrigan.

The expression, "Dear Entire Alphabet—" (pg 27) is taken from Dina Hardy, with permission, as is her poem which makes up the first passage of the fictional "double epigraph" on page 19:

> "'How your name remains tattooed below the faded tan
> line on my hipbone. Z. No longer part of the Icelandic
> alphabet, and hasn't always been the final letter of the
> English. Once, it was second to last, followed by an
> ampersand: like this chiasmic attempt to return to where
> we started—&, &, &, &.'"

The poems in this text, or earlier versions of them, have appeared/will soon appear in the following journals:

"(Day 700)," *The Colorado Review*
"(Day 33)" and "(Day 111)," *The Offing*
"[Picture of a crowd...]," *Timber*
"(Day 1,500,000)," *small po[r]tions*
"(Day 49)," *Tupelo Quarterly* (TQ7 semifinalist)
"(Day 0)," *Talking Writing*
"(Day 105)," *Electric Literature, Okey-Panky*
"[the loneliness of a middle distance transmissions aggregator...],"
    Bayou Magazine
    -Winner, Kay Murphy Prize; nominated, Pushcart Prize
"(Day—)," *Hardy Doughnuts*
    -Nominated, Best New Poets, 2016
"[a notebook bound with cassette tape...]." *Fjords* (excerpt)

Most of the interstitial pages containing a single line of text were collected under the title "car money snacks mixtape gun," and published in *TYPO*.

Marco Maisto is a contumbled list, a rogue signal, a stamped envelope with pieces of two-way mirror inside, and a writer interested in the natural history of future qualities. His work explores the emotional landscape of conceivable worlds.

He was educated at the University of Chicago and the Iowa Writer's Workshop and has been a contributing and guest editor for Drunken Boat, co-curating their poetry comics and animation folio with Michael Chaney. Marco's long poem, "The Loneliness of the Middle-Distance Transmissions Aggregator," (*Bayou Magazine*) was nominated for a Pushcart Prize. Parts of *Traces of a Fifth Column,* his first full-length book, have been published in *Electric Literature, Okey Panky, The Colorado Review, Fjords, The Offing, jubilat, small po[r]tions, TYPO, Pangyrus* and other fine outlets.

More of his written and visual work can be found at telepathicsyntax.com, @MarcoMaisto (twitter) and @networkbreakdown (Instagram).

Marco lives in New York City.

CPSIA information can be obtained
at www.ICGtesting.com
Printed in the USA
BVOW03s1401050717

488460BV00042B/194/P